AIR FRYER RECIPE

For Quick and Healthy Meals

Table of Contents

As a way of saying thank you for purchasing my book, please use your link below to claim your 3 FREE Cookbooks on Health, Fitness & Dieting Instantly

https://bit.ly/2uS1BhB

You can also share your link with your friends and families whom you think that can benefit from the cookbooks or you can forward them the link as a gift!

Introduction

The following chapters will discuss some of the many of the reasons why the air fryer is worth the investment. Your air fryer can bake, roast, and grill your favorite foods. From the Breakfast Burrito to the tasty Fried Pickles, you will be sure to enjoy every morsel.

Throughout your experiences with your Air Fryer; you may have the need to have these conversion charts to make sure you have the correct measurements for your healthy dishes.

- **Grams to Cups:**
  http://www.convertunits.com/from/grams/to/cups

- **Grams to Pounds:**
  http://www.rapidtables.com/convert/weight/gram-to-pound.htm

- **Celsius to Fahrenheit:**
  http://www.rapidtables.com/convert/temperature/celsius-to-fahrenheit.htm

- **Milliliters to Cups:**
  http://www.metric-conversions.org/volume/milliliters-to-cups.htm

There are plenty of books on this subject on the market, thanks again for choosing this one! Every effort was made to ensure it is full of as much useful information as possible. You will discover many new ways to enjoy breakfast, lunch, and dinner. Don't forget the yummy snacks; they are all here.

Please enjoy!

CHAPTER 1

Breakfast Recipes

Apple Dumplings

Ingredients

1 tbsp. brown sugar

2 small apples

2 tbsp. of each:

-Raisins

-Melted butter

2 sheets puff pastry

Directions

1. Program the Air Fryer to 356ºF.

2. Peel and remove the core of the apples. Mix the sugar and raisins. Arrange each apple on one of the pastry sheets and fill with the sugar and raisins mixture.

3. Fold the pastry over until the apple and raisins are fully covered. Place them onto a piece of foil. Brush them with the melted butter.

4. Set the time for 25 minutes and cook until browned to your liking.

Yields: 1-2 Servings

Baked Eggs in a Bread Bowl

Ingredients

4 large eggs

4 dinner rolls – crusty

4 tbsp. of each:

  -Heavy cream

  -Mixed herbs – for ex. Chopped tarragon, chives parsley

Grated parmesan cheese

Directions

1. Program the air fryer to 350ºF.

2. Use a sharp knife to remove the top of each of the rolls – setting the tops aside for later. Scoop out some of the bread to form a hole large enough for the egg.

3. Place the rolls in the fryer basket. Break an egg into the roll and top with the cream and herbs. Sprinkle with some parmesan.

4. Bake for about 20-25 minutes until the egg is set. The bread should be toasted.

5. After 20 minutes, arrange the tops of the bread on the egg and bake a few more minutes to finish the browning process.

6. Let the eggs rest for five minutes. Serve warm.

Yields: 4 Egg Bowls

Breakfast Burrito

Ingredients

2 eggs

3-4 slices chicken or turkey breast

¼ sliced avocado

¼ sliced bell pepper

1/8 c. mozzarella cheese – grated

Pinch of pepper and salt

2 tbsp. salsa

1 tortilla

Directions

1. In a small mixing dish, whisk the eggs, and add salt and pepper to your liking.

2. Add the mixture into a small pan/tin and arrange it in the AF basket.

3. Cook for five minutes at 392ºF.

4. When done, transfer the egg from the pan and fill the tortilla. Combine all of the ingredients and wrap it, but don't over-stuff.

5. Add a piece of foil to the AF tray and add the burrito.

6. Heat for three minutes at 356ºF.

7. The cheese will be melted and the tortilla crispy. Garnish as desired and enjoy!

8. Yields: 1-2 Servings

Breakfast Frittata

Ingredients

½ of 1 Italian sausage

3 eggs

1 tbsp. olive oil

4 cherry tomatoes – cut into halves

Parmesan cheese

Chopped parsley

Salt and pepper as desired

Also Needed:

Non-stick baking dish

Directions

1. Set the temperature to 360ºF.

2. Add the sausage and tomatoes to the baking pan and cook for five minutes.

3. In a separate container, whisk together the remainder of ingredients.

4. Remove the AF basket and add the eggs – spreading evenly.

5. Add back to the fryer and cook for five more minutes.

Yields: 1-2 Servings

French Toast Sticks

Ingredients

2 gently beaten eggs

2 tbsp. soft butter/margarine

4 slices of bread

Cinnamon

Salt

Ground cloves

Nutmeg

Icing sugar or maple syrup – or both

Cooking spray

Directions

1. Set the temperature on the air fryer to 356ºF.

2. Gently whisk the eggs along with the nutmeg, cloves, cinnamon, and salt.

3. Add butter to both sides of the bread and slice into strips.

4. Lightly dredge the sticks into the egg mix and add to the basket of the air fryer.

5. Pause the fryer after two minutes, remove the pan, and add some cooking spray to the slices. Flip them over and spray the other side. (It may take two batches.)

6. Cook for four minutes making sure not to burn them.

Remove when the egg is browned and serve right away.

7. Garnish with some syrup, a sprinkle of sugar, or another garnish to your liking.

Yields: 2 Servings

Sausage Wraps

Ingredients

1 can crescent roll dough (8 count)

2 slices American cheese

8 Heat & Serve Sausages

8 wooden skewers

For Dipping: Ketchup, syrup, or BBQ sauce

Directions

1. Cut the cheese into quarters. Open the sausages, and separate the rolls.

2. Add the cheese strips starting on the widest part of the triangle to the tip. Add the sausage.

3. Pull up each of the ends of the roll over the sausage and cheese. Be sure to pinch all of the sides together and add these in two batches to the air fryer.

4. Set the AF to 380ºF. Cook for three minutes, maybe four depending on how crispy you like the bread.

5. Remove from the fryer and add a skewer. Set it out for serving with the desired garnish.

Yields: 8 Wraps

CHAPTER 2

Lunch Recipes

All-Time Grill Cheese Sandwich

Ingredients

2 t. butter

2 slices sandwich bread

2-3 slices cheddar cheese

Directions

1. Add the slices of cheese to the bread.
2. Spread butter on the outside of the sandwich.
3. Set the air fryer to 370ºF for eight minutes.
4. Flip once at four minutes.
5. Transfer to a dish and enjoy.

Yields: 1 Serving

Hot Dogs

Ingredients

2 hot dogs

2 buns for the hot dogs

2 tbsp. grated cheese

Directions

1. Allow the air fryer to warm up for four minutes at 390ºF.

2. Arrange the hot dogs in the fryer and cook for five minutes or until done.

3. Transfer from the cooker to the bun and garnish with cheese.

4. Place the prepared dog in the fryer for about two minutes to melt the cheese.

Yields: 2 Servings

Pita Bread Cheese Pizza

Ingredients

1 tbsp. pizza sauce

1 drizzle extra-virgin olive oil

¼ c. mozzarella cheese

1 pita bread

Also Needed: 1 stainless steel short legged trivet

Ingredients for the Toppings

¼ c. sausage

7 slices pepperoni

½ tsp. fresh minced garlic

1 tbsp. sliced onions

Directions

1. Swirl the sauce onto the pita bread. Add your chosen toppings and cheese.

2. Give it a drizzle of oil and add to a trivet in the air fryer.

3. Bake for six minutes at 350ºF.

4. When done and browned, transfer to a dish and slice to serve.

Yields: 1 Serving

Roast Pork Loin with Red Potatoes

Ingredients

2 large red potatoes

2 pounds pork loin

1 t. of each:

   -Pepper

   -Salt

   -Parsley

½ t. of each:

   -Red pepper flakes

   -Garlic powder

Balsamic glaze from cooking

Directions

1. Dice the potatoes.
2. Combine all of the seasonings and sprinkle over the potatoes and loin.
3. Arrange the pork and then the potatoes in the air fryer.
4. Secure the top and choose the roast button. Set the timer for 25 minutes.
5. When done, let it rest for several minutes before slicing.
6. Meanwhile, pour the roasted potatoes into the serving dishes.
7. Slice the loin into 4-5 sections. Use a balsamic glaze over the pork.

Yields: 2 Servings

Roast Turkey Reuben

Ingredients

4 slices rye bread

8 slices skinless – roasted turkey breast

4 tbsp. coleslaw

8 slices swiss cheese

2 tbsp. each of:

-Salted butter

-Russian dressing

Directions

1. Prepare two slices of the bread on one side with butter and lay them – butter side down- on the cutting board.

2. In layers, arrange the turkey, cheese, coleslaw, and Russian dressing on top of the two slices of bread. Fold them together to make one sandwich.

3. Add the sandwich to the air fryer basket.

4. Push 'm' and choose the bake icon setting it to 310ºF for 12 minutes.

5. After six minutes, flip the sandwich, and continue until browned.

6. When done, slice and serve.

Yields: 2 Servings

Stromboli

Ingredients

1 pizza crust – 12 ounces – refrigerated is easiest

¾ c. shredded mozzarella cheese

1/3 lb. sliced cooked ham

3 c. shredded cheddar cheese

1 egg yolk

1 tbsp. milk

3 ounces roasted red bell peppers

Directions

1. Prepare the dough for a ¼-inch thickness.

2. Add the ham, peppers, and cheese on one side of the dough.

3. Fold the dough over the ingredients and pinch together.

4. Make a wash with the milk and egg. Brush the top of the dough.

5. Arrange the prepared Stromboli in the basket.

6. Press the 'm' button and use the chicken icon. Cook at 360ºF for 15 minutes. Observe as it cooks, and flip each five-minute segment.

Yields: 4 Servings

CHAPTER 3

Beef Recipes

Beef Roll Ups

Ingredients

6 slices provolone cheese

2 lbs. beef flank steak

3 tablespoons pesto

¾ c. fresh baby spinach

3 ounces roasted red bell peppers

1 tsp. of each:

   -Black pepper

   -Sea salt

Directions

1. Open the steak (4 pieces) and spread the pesto, layer the cheese, spinach, and peppers (¾ down the meat).

2. Roll it up and secure it with toothpicks. Sprinkle the roll up with some salt and pepper.

3. Program the AF to 400ºF. Cook the roll ups 14 minutes, rotating halfway through the process.

4. Let them rest ten minutes before you slice and serve.

Yields: 4 Servings

Country Fried Steak

Ingredients

1 (6-ounce) sirloin steak

3 beaten eggs

1 c. of each:

-Panko

-Flour

1 tsp. of each:

-Pepper

-Salt

-Garlic powder

-Onion powder

6 ounces ground sausage

2 tbsp. flour

1 tsp. pepper

2 c. milk

Directions

1. Pound the steak until thin. Add the seasonings with the panko.

2. First, dredge the beef in the flour, then the egg, and lastly the panko.

3. Arrange the steak in the basket. Set the temperature to 370ºF. It should take 12 minutes. Remove the steak

and enjoy with some mashed potatoes and gravy.

4. *For the Gravy*: Cook the sausage and drain (Save two tablespoons in the pan). Blend in the flour along with the sausage and mix well.

5. Pour in the milk and stir until thickened. Add more pepper and cook about three more minutes.

Yields: 1 Serving

Hamburgers in the Air Fryer

Ingredients

1 lb. 93% lean ground beef

Few drops liquid smoke

1 tsp. of each:

-Dried parsley

-Maggi seasoning sauce

½ tsp. of each:

-Onion powder

-Garlic powder

-Ground black pepper

-Salt substitute

-Dried oregano

Directions

1. Lightly spray the air fryer with cooking oil. If basket type, no need to spray. Set the temperature to 350ºF.

2. Combine all of the seasonings in a small dish and add to the beef in a large mixing container. Don't over-work the meat because it will become tough.

3. Prepare four patties and make a thumb indention to keep the patties from bunching up in the center. Place the burgers in the air fryer for ten minutes for medium doneness. You don't need to turn the patties.

4. When done, arrange and add the desired garnishes on a bun.

Yields: 4 Servings

Meatloaf with Black Peppercorns

Ingredients

4 ½ pounds minced beef

3 tbsp. tomato ketchup

1 large onion – diced

1 tsp Worcestershire sauce

1 tbsp. of each:

   -Parsley

   -Basil

   -Oregano

Pinch of salt and pepper

Breadcrumbs – if homemade one slice of bread

Directions

1. Add the beef into a large mixing container. Toss in the onion, Worcestershire sauce, herbs, and ketchup. Blend well for about five minutes.

2. Add the crumbs and mix well.

3. Arrange the meatloaf in the baking dish and place in the air fryer.

4. Cook for 25 minutes at 356ºF.

Yields: 4 Servings

Air Fried Rib Eye Steak

Ingredients

1 tbsp. olive oil

1 steak – approx. 2 lbs.

1 tbsp. steak rub/to Taste: Salt and pepper

Baking pan also needed to fit into the basket

Directions

1. Let the steak rest a few minutes while you set the temperature setting on the air fryer. Press the 'M' button for the French Fries icon. Adjust the time to four minutes at 400ºF.

2. Rub the steak with the oil and seasonings.

3. Add the steak to the basket and cook for 14 minutes. (After seven minutes, flip the steak.)

4. Transfer the steak to the serving dish and let it rest for ten minutes. Slice it and garnish the way you like it.

Yields: 1 Serving

CHAPTER 4

Chicken Recipes

Buffalo Chicken Wings

Ingredients

14 ounces chicken wings – approx. 5 wings

2 tablespoons red hot sauce

1 tablespoon melted butter

2 teaspoons cayenne pepper

Fresh black pepper

To Taste: Salt

Optional: ½ teaspoon garlic powder

Directions

1. Program the Air Fryer temperature to 356ºF.

2. Slice the wings into three sections - the drumstick, middle joint, and end tip. Dry each piece completely.

3. Blend the garlic powder, pepper, salt, and cayenne pepper in a mixing dish. Cover the wings.

4. Arrange the chicken on the wire rack and bake for 15 minutes. Flip it once about ½ through the cooking cycle.

5. Mix the hot sauce and butter in a dish. Garnish the baked chicken when ready to be served.

Yields: 2 Servings

Chicken Fried Rice

Ingredients

1 c. frozen carrots and peas

3 c. cold cooked white rice

1 tbsp. vegetable oil

6 tbsp. soy sauce

1 c. – packed cooked chicken

½ c. diced onion

Also Needed: 7x2 cake pan

Directions

1. Cook and dice the chicken. Prepare the rice. Dice the onion.

2. Add the chilled white rice into a mixing container along with the soy sauce and oil. Mix well.

3. Toss in the onion, chicken, peas, and carrots. Mix well.

4. Combine the ingredients in the air fryer and cook 20 minutes at 360ºF.

5. Serve as a side with your favorite meat or enjoy it alone.

Yields: 5-6 Servings

Chicken Kabobs

Ingredients

3 bell peppers – multi colors

6 mushrooms

1/3 c. each of:

   -Soy sauce

   -Honey

To taste: Pepper and salt

Cooking oil spray

Sesame seeds

2 diced chicken breasts

Directions

1. Chop the mushrooms into halves. Dice the chicken and peppers. Give the chicken a couple squirts of oil and a pinch of salt and pepper.

2. Combine the soy and honey – mixing well. Add some sesame seeds and stir.

3. Insert the peppers, chicken, and mushroom bits onto a skewer.

4. Set the temperature of the air fryer to 338ºF. Cover the kabobs with the sauce and add them to the AF basket.

5. Cook for 15-20 minutes and serve.

Yields: 2 Servings

Chicken Kiev Supper

Ingredients

1 medium chicken breast

3 ½ ounces soft cheese

¼ t. garlic puree

1 medium beaten egg

1 t. parsley

Breadcrumbs

Pepper and salt to taste

Directions

1. Combine the garlic, soft cheese, and ½ of the parsley.

2. Flatten the breast of chicken. Chop into two pieces to have a top and bottom for stuffing.

3. Use the goodies (step 1) and place in the center putting the breasts together (sandwich style).

4. Combine the remainder of the parsley, pepper, salt, and breadcrumbs in a mixing container.

5. Coat the chicken with the beaten egg and roll it in the crumbs.

6. Prepare the air fryer to 356ºF and cook for 25 minutes.

7. When the chicken is done, serve, and enjoy.

Yields: 2 Servings

Chicken Pot Pie

Ingredients

6 chicken tenders

2 potatoes

1 ½ c. condensed cream of celery soup

¾ c. heavy cream

1 sprig of thyme

1 whole dried bay leaf

5 refrigerated buttermilk biscuits

1 tbsp. milk

1 egg yolk

Directions

1. Set the temperature to the Air Fryer at 320ºF.

2. Peel the potatoes and dice.

3. Mix all of the components in a pan except for the egg yolk, milk, and biscuits. Let it boil over medium heat. Empty the mix into the baking pan and cover the top. Arrange the pan into the fry basket. Set the timer for 15 minutes.

4. After the pie is done, make an egg wash with the milk and egg yolk. Put the biscuits onto the baking tray and brush with the egg wash mixture.

5. Set the timer and cook for an additional ten minutes at 300ºF.

Yields: 4 Servings

Orange Chicken Wings

Ingredients

1 orange – zest and juiced

6 chicken wings

1 ½ tbsp. Worcestershire sauce

1 tbsp. sugar

Herbs: Sage, thyme, basil, mint, parsley, oregano, etc.

Pepper

Directions

1. Prepare the wings and pour the juice and zest into a bowl with the wings.

2. Add the remainder of the ingredients and rub in. Let it marinate for 30 minutes.

3. Program the temperature on the Air Fryer to 356ºF.

4. Combine the wings and juices together. Add to the fryer basket for 20 minutes.

5. Remove the wings from the fryer and discard the zest and brush ½ of the sauce over the wings. Return to the fryer and cook an additional ten minutes.

6. Add the wings to a serving platter and enjoy!

Yields: 2 Servings

CHAPTER 5

Fish and Seafood Recipes

Cajun Salmon

Ingredients

1 salmon fillet – approx. 200 g. – ¾-inches thick

Juice of ¼ lemon

Cajun seasoning for coating

Optional: Sprinkle of sugar

Directions

1. Preheat the AF to 356ºF. The process usually takes about five minutes.

2. Rinse and pat the salmon dry. Thoroughly coat the fish with the coating mix.

3. Arrange the fillet in the fryer for seven minutes with the skin side up.

4. Serve with a sprinkle of the lemon.

Yields: 1-2 Servings

Crumbled Fish

Ingredients

½ cup breadcrumbs

4 tablespoons vegetable oil

1 whisked egg

4 fish fillets

To Serve: 1 lemon

Directions

1. Heat the air fryer unit to 356ºF.

2. Mix the oil and breadcrumbs until it is crumbly. Dip the fish into the egg, then the crumb mix.

3. Arrange it in the fryer and cook for 12 minutes. Garnish with the lemon.

Yields: 2 Servings

Fish Tacos

Ingredients

1 c. tempura batter – made from:

-1 c. flour

-1 tbsp. cornstarch

½ c. of each:

-Cold seltzer water

-Salsa

1 c. coleslaw

1 teaspoon white pepper

2 tbsp. chopped cilantro

½ c. guacamole

1 lemon – wedges

Directions

1. Prepare the tempura batter. Add a pinch of salt to the mixture to make it smooth.
2. Slice the cod into two-ounce pieces and give them a sprinkle of salt and pepper.
3. Use the batter (step 1) to coat the cod. Dredge them in the panko.
4. Use the French fry setting and cook for ten minutes. Turn after five minutes.
5. Garnish with some of the coleslaw, guacamole, cilantro, salsa, or some lemon.

Yields: 6 Servings

Cod Steaks with Ginger

Ingredients

2 slices large cod steaks

Pinch of pepper and salt

½ teaspoon of each:

   -Ginger powder

   -Garlic powder

¼ teaspoon turmeric powder

1 tablespoon plum sauce

Ginger slices

1 part of corn flour (plus) 1 part of Kentucky Kernel Seasoned Flour

Directions

1. Pat the cod steaks dry with some towels. Marinate with the ginger powder, pepper, salt, and turmeric powder for a few minutes.

2. Coat each of the steaks with the corn flour and Kentucky mix.

3. Program the temperature in the air fryer to 356ºF for 15 minutes and increase to 400ºF for five minutes.

4. Prepare the sauce in a wok. Brown the ginger slices and remove from the heat. Add the plum sauce. You can dilute the sauce with a small amount of water if desired. Serve the steaks with a drizzle of the tasty sauce.

Yields: 2 Servings

Lemon Fish

Ingredients

2 Basa/catfish cut into 4 pieces

Juice of 1 lemon

¼ c. sugar

2 tsp. green chili sauce

Salt to taste

1 egg white

4 tsp. corn flour slurry

1 tsp. red chili sauce

2-3 lettuce leaves

For Brushing: 2 tsp. oil

Directions

1. Boil ½ cup of water in a pan and add the sugar. Slice the lemon and place it in a dish.

2. Add the egg white, two teaspoons of oil, green sauce, salt, and flour in a bowl, mixing well. Add three tablespoons of water and whisk to make a smooth slurry batter.

3. Add some flour to a plate. Dip in the batter and then the flour.

4. Lightly grease the air fryer basket with a little oil and heat to 356ºF.

5. Arrange the fillets in the basket and cook for 15-20

minutes until crispy.

6. Add salt to the pan (step 2) and stir well. Add the corn flour slurry and mix again. Blend in the red sauce juice, and lemon slices, mixing well and cooking until thickened.

7. Remove the fish from the basket, brush with some oil, and place back into the pan. Cook for about five more minutes.

8. Tear the leaves apart to make a serving bed. Add the fish and pour the lemon sauce over the top of the fish.

9. Devour the tasty treat!

Yields: 4 Servings

Salmon Patties

Ingredients

1 salmon portion – approx. 1 ounce

3 large russet potatoes

1 handful frozen vegetables

2 dill sprinkles

Chopped parsley

Pinch of black pepper

1 egg

To Taste: Salt

Breadcrumbs – Panko or 4 bread slices

Cooking spray – olive oil

Directions

1. Peel and dice the potatoes. Parboil for ten minutes, and drain the veggies.

2. Add the potatoes back into the cooking pot over a low burner setting for about two to three minutes. Smash them and place in the fridge to chill.

3. Prepare the breadcrumbs, by breaking the bread into bits and set to the side.

4. Program the air fryer temperature to 356ºF to warm for five minutes.

5. Air fry the salmon for five minutes.

6. Combine the parboiled veggies and the refrigerated

potatoes along with the salt, pepper, dill, parsley, and flaked salmon.

7. Arrange the salmon mixture into either six or eight patties.

8. Coat the patties with bread crumbs. Use some of the oil spray to coat the crumbs to make sure they have a nice color.

9. Cook 8-10 minutes in the AF at 356ºF.

10. Enjoy with some lemon, mayo, or a side salad.

Yields: 6-8 Patties

CHAPTER 6

Side Dishes

Buffalo Cauliflower

Ingredients

4 c. florets

1 c. panko breadcrumbs (plus) 1 tsp. of sea salt

¼ c. of each for the coating:

   -Melted butter

   -Buffalo sauce

To Dip: Your choice of a creamy dressing

Directions

1. Put the butter in the microwave to melt, and add it to the buffalo sauce.

2. Dip each of the florets in the mixture, letting it drip the excess off before dredging it through the panko mixture.

3. Arrange each of the florets in the fryer. Cook until crispy for 14-17 minutes at 350ºF.

4. Enjoy with your dipping sauce.

Yield: 4 Servings

Button Mushroom Melt

Ingredients

Button mushrooms – 10

Italian dried mixed herbs

Salt and pepper

Mozzarella cheese

Cheddar cheese

Optional Garnish: Dried dill

Directions

1. Wash the mushrooms, remove the stems, and let drain.

2. Flavor with a pinch of black pepper, salt, herbs, and olive oil.

3. Heat the air fryer ahead of time to 356ºF. About three to five minutes should be okay.

4. Add the mushrooms to the basket with the hollow section facing you. Sprinkle the cheese on top of each of the caps.

5. Add the mushrooms to the cooker for seven to eight minutes.

6. Serve piping hot with a drizzle of basil or other herbs.

Yields: 10 Mushrooms

Grilled Corn with Feta and Lime

Ingredients

2 tsp. paprika

2 whole-corn on the cob

Olive oil

½ c. grated feta cheese

2-3 small limes

Directions

1. Remove the corn husks and silks. Use the olive oil to rub down the corn. Sprinkle with some paprika and work in well using your hands.

2. Warm up the air fryer to 392ºF.

3. Arrange the prepared corn into the basket/grill pan.

4. Program the timer for 12-15 minutes. Adjust the time as need if it is cooking too fast.

5. Remove the corn from the AF when done.

6. Grate some frozen feta cheese over the corn.

7. Drizzle with some lime juice and serve.

Yields: 2 Servings/2 Ears

Homemade Croutons

Ingredients

Butter – salted or unsalted

Stale bread

Optional: Olive oil

Directions

1. Set the Air Fryer to 284ºF for two to three minutes.

2. Cut up the stale bread into the desired size for your recipe.

3. Toss in the oil and melted butter. Empty the cubed bread into the cooker.

4. Cook for two to three minutes. Toss and cook for an additional two to three minutes.

5. Once the croutons are cooled, you can store them in a closed container.

Yields: Your choice

Garlic Knots

Ingredients

1 lb. crust – frozen dough is easiest

½ c. olive oil

1 t. salt

1 tbsp. of each:

-Garlic

-Fresh chopped parsley

-Grated parmesan cheese

On the Side: Marinara sauce

Directions

1. Roll out the dough and slice lengthwise making the slice about ¾-inch apart. Roll out each section and make a knot of the dough.

2. Add all of the spices, oil, and cheese in a container and mix well. Roll the knots in the mixture and add to the fryer.

3. Press the 'M' button to the chicken icon. Adjust the timing for 12 minutes at 360ºF. Flip the knots about ½ way through the process.

4. Serve with some marinara sauce if you desire.

Yields: 4 Servings

Stuffed Mushrooms with Sour Cream

Ingredients

2 rashers of bacon (bacon with meat and fat strips)

½ green pepper

1 small carrot

1 c. grated cheese

½ c. sour cream

24 medium-sized mushrooms -

Directions

1. Remove the mushroom stalks. Dice the onion, carrots, bacon, and the mushroom stalks.

2. Saute the veggies and bacon bits in a pan until softened. Add the cheese and sour cream. Mixing well to incorporate.

3. Heat the fryer for five minutes at 356ºF. Cook for 8 minutes.

Yields: 24 Mushrooms

Twice Baked Loaded Air-Fried Potatoes

Ingredients

1 t. olive oil

1 potato – 14-16 ounces

1 tbsp. each of:

  -Finely chopped green onion

  -Unsalted butter

2 tbsp. heavy cram

1/8 t. black pepper

¼ t. salt

Directions

1. Cook the bacon about ten minutes - reserving the fat - and chop into ½-inch pieces.

2. Finely chop the onions.

3. Coat the potato with the oil and add to the AF basket. Set the temperature to 400ºF for 30 minutes. Add a little more oil to the fryer, turn the potato, and cook another 30 minutes. Cool for a minimum of 20 minutes.

4. When cooled, slice the potato lengthways. Scoop out the pulp leaving about ¼-inch borders to support the filling.

5. Whisk together the scooped potato along with the bacon fat, bacon bits, ¼ cup of the cheese, 1 ½ tsp of the onions, pepper, salt, butter, and lastly the cream. Combine well.

6. Scoop the mixture into the prepared skins. Garnish with the cheese and place them in the air fryer.

7. Set the timer for 20 minutes or until the tops are browned, and the cheese is melted.

8. Sprinkle the rest of the onions on top of the potato and serve.

Yields: 2 Servings

CHAPTER 7

Vegetable Recipes

Broccoli

Ingredients

2 tbsp. olive oil

2 lbs. broccoli florets

1 tsp. kosher salt

¼ c. shaved parmesan cheese

1/3 c. Kalamata olives

2 tsp. grated lemon zest

½ tsp. black pepper

Directions

1. Remove the stems from the broccoli and chop them into one-inch florets. Discard the olive pits and slice them into halves.

2. Fill a saucepan (high heat) with six cups of water. When it begins to boil, toss in the florets, and continue cooking for about three to four minutes. Drain and add the oil, salt, and pepper. Stir gently.

3. Prepare the temperature setting to 400ºF.

4. Arrange the broccoli in the basket, shut the AF drawer, and set the timer for 15 minutes. Turn the broccoli over at seven minutes to ensure even browning.

5. Garnish with olives, lemon zest, and cheese.

Yields: 2-4 Servings

AF Chickpeas – Ranch & Vegan Style

Ingredients

1 batch homemade ranch seasoning (see below)

1 can unrinsed chickpeas – drained

1 t. sea salt

2 tbsp. of each:

   -Olive oil – divided

   -Lemon juice

Directions

1. Combine one tablespoon of the oil in a small dish along with the chickpeas. Air fry for 15 minutes at 400ºF.

2. Empty the peas back into the dish and blend in the rest of the oil plus the prepared ranch seasoning, lemon juice, and salt. Be sure the beans are well coated.

3. Arrange the chickpeas back into the fryer basket. Cook for five more minutes at 350ºF. Enjoy and store any leftovers in an airtight container. They will be yummy for a couple of days on the counter.

For the Ranch Seasoning

2 tsp. of each:

   -Garlic powder

   -Onion powder

4 tsp. dried dill

Directions

1. Combine all of the ingredients in a small dish.

Yields: 4 Servings

Hasselback Potatoes

Ingredients

Olive oil

4 peeled potatoes

Directions

2. Peel the potatoes and slice into halves. Cut slits about 1/16-inches apart from the base. Be careful to not cut all the way through to make the feathered effect.

3. Set the temperature of the air fryer to 356ºF.

4. Gently brush the potatoes with oil and arrange them into the fryer for 15 minutes. Remove and brush again cooking for about 15 additional minutes or until browned and cooked all the way through.

Yields: 4 Servings

Honey Roasted Carrots

Ingredients

3 c. carrots

1 tbsp. of each:

-Honey

-Olive oil

To Taste: Salt and pepper

Directions

1. Cut the carrots into small chunks or use some baby carrots.

2. Combine the oil, honey, and carrots in a mixing dish, making sure they are fully coated.

3. Sprinkle with some pepper and salt.

4. Arrange the carrots in the air fryer and cook at 392ºF for 12 minutes.

Yield: 4 Servings

Mediterranean Vegetables

Ingredients

¼ c. cherry tomatoes

1 medium carrot

1 green pepper

1 large parsnip

1 large cucumber

2 tbsp. of each:

   -Garlic puree

   -Honey

6 tbsp. olive oil

1 tsp. mixed herbs

To Taste: Pepper and salt

Directions

1. Chop the cucumber and green pepper and add it to the bottom of the air fryer.

2. Peel and dice the carrot and parsnip, adding the whole cherry tomatoes.

3. Drizzle with three tablespoons of oil and cook at 356ºF for 15 minutes.

4. Mix the rest of the ingredients in an 'air fryer safe' baking dish.

5. Add the veggies to the marinade and shake well. Give it a sprinkle of pepper and salt, and cook at 392ºF for

another five minutes.

6. *Note*: You can substitute and experiment with different veggies, but don't use the cucumber and cauliflower in the same dish. Together, they produce too much liquid.

7. Serve and enjoy. You can also add some honey and sweet potatoes to the mixture.

Yields: 4 Servings

Onion Rings

Ingredients

1 large onion – approx. 14 ounces

¼ c. egg whites

¼ t. salt

2/3 c. whole wheat panko breadcrumbs

1 t. of each:

-Garlic powder

-Onion powder

2 tbsp. whole wheat flour

1/8 t. black pepper

Directions

1. Cut away the ends and outer layer of the onion. Slice into 1/-inch slices and separate them into rings.
2. Whisk the egg whites in a small dish.
3. Combine the seasonings and breadcrumbs in another bowl.
4. Add some flour and the rings into a plastic bag and shake to cover the rings evenly. Coat them with the egg whites and the breadcrumb mixture.
5. Add the coated rings to the air fryer at 392ºF.
6. Bake for about six minutes or to your liking.

Yields: 2 Servings

Air Fried Potato Wedges

Ingredients

1 tbsp. vegetable oil

2 large potatoes

Sour cream

Sweet chili sauce

Directions

1. Slice the potatoes in a uniform pattern into either eights or twelfths.

2. Program the AF to 356ºF.

3. Empty the oil into a plastic bag and add the potatoes. Shake the bag to coat the potatoes. Dump the contents of the bag into the fryer.

4. Cook for 15 minutes, toss the wedges in the basket and return to the fryer. Cook another ten minutes until well done.

5. Garnish as desired.

Yields: 4 Servings

CHAPTER 8

Snacks and Appetizers

Apple Chips

Ingredients

1 apple

½ t. ground cinnamon

1 tbsp. sugar

Pinch of salt

Directions

1. Core and thinly slice the apple – horizontally.

2. Program the air fryer to 390ºF ahead of time.

3. Prepare the apples on a cookie sheet with the combined spice mixture of salt, sugar, and cinnamon.

4. It may take more than one batch. Arrange the slices in the basket of the fryer. Cook until each one is browned – usually about seven to eight minutes. Flip them once during the cooking time.

5. Add the chips to a serving platter and cool. Serve it with a dip or other desired garnish.

Yields: 2 Servings

Avocado Fries

Ingredients

1 Haas avocado

½ c. panko breadcrumbs

½ t. salt

Aquafaba from 1 can – 15.oz. garbanzo/white beans

Directions

1. Peel, pit, and slice the avocado.

2. Combine the salt and panko in a shallow container.

3. In another shallow dish, pour the aquafaba that you drained from the beans.

4. Use a dredging system with the avocado. Run the slices through the aquafaba, and then the panko to make an even cover.

5. Place the slices evenly in the fryer basket.

6. No need to preheat. Air fry for ten minutes at 390ºF.

7. Shake the basket after about five minutes.

8. Enjoy with your favorite sauce.

Note: This is also a vegan favorite.

Yields: 4 Servings

Cheesy Garlic Bread

Ingredients

3 chopped garlic cloves

5 slices – round bread - ex. baquette bread

4 tbsp. melted butte

5 tsp. sun dried tomato pesto

1 c. grated mozzarella cheese

Garnishes:

-Chili flakes

-Chopped basil leaves

-Oregano

Directions

1. Add the garlic cloves with the butter.

2. Slice the bread into five thick round slices.

3. Spread the butter on each of the slices. Sprinkle a healthy amount on each slice of buttered toast.

4. Bake the bread in the fryer at 356ºF for six to eight minutes.

Yields: 5 Slices

Churro Doughnut Holes

Ingredients

1 c. all-purpose white flour

¼ c. of each:

   -Organic (if vegan) sugar

   -Almond/soy milk

½ t. salt

1 t. baking powder

¼ t. cinnamon

2 tbsp. aquafaba – liquid from chickpeas

1 tbsp. melted coconut oil

2 t. cinnamon

2 tbsp. sugar

Directions

1. In a large mixing container, comb ine the salt, cinnamon, flour, baking powder, and sugar.

2. Add the coconut oil soy milk, and aquafaba (from the beans). Mix with forks and knead with your hands to form the dough for a few seconds. You will have a sticky dough. Place the dough in the fridge for a minimum of one hour. Be sure it is in an airtight container, since you can let it rest overnight.

3. Combine the rest of the sugar with the cinnamon, setting aside until later.

4. Partially cover the bottom of the air fryer with parchment paper. Leave a space of about one-inch smaller than the lower portion of the air fryer.

5. Transfer the cold bread to the counter and divide it into 12 balls.

6. Run each of the balls through the sugar and cinnamon. Place them in one layer - leaving the one-inch space for air to circulate. Two batches of six are the easiest way to prepare the donuts.

7. Heat up the AF to 370ºF. Cook for six minutes. Do not shake because the donuts will crumble.

8. Let them cool for five to ten minutes. The times can vary depending on the fryer size.

Yields: 6 Servings

Corn Tortilla Chips

Ingredients

1 tbsp. olive oil

Salt if desired

8 corn tortillas

Directions

1. Set the temperature on the air fryer to 392ºF.

2. Cut the tortillas into chip sizes, and brush each one with oil.

3. Air fry two batches for three minutes each.

4. Serve warm and enjoy.

Yields: 2 Servings

Crispy Fried Pickles

Ingredients

¼ c. all-purpose flour

1/8 t. baking powder

14 thinly sliced dill pickles – refrigerated & crunchy

Pinch of salt

3 tbsp. dark beer (German beer is vegan.)

2-3 tbsp. water

6 tbsp. panko breadcrumbs

2 tbsp. cornstarch

Pinch of cayenne pepper

½ t. paprika

For Frying: Organic canola or oil spray

¼-1/2 cup ranch dressing

Directions

1. Use paper towels to dry the pickles. Set to the side for later.

2. Mix the beer, two tablespoons of water, a pinch of salt, baking powder, and flour. Its consistency should be similar to waffle batter.

3. Prepare two platters. One will have the cornstarch, and the other will have a pinch of salt, the cayenne, paprika, and breadcrumbs.

4. Bread the pickles. Prepare the working surface with

the pickles, cornstarch, beer batter, and panko mixture.

5. Dip each of the pickles into the cornstarch and remove excess starch. Dip each one into the batter until evenly covered. Let the excess batter drip away. Lastly, add the pickle into the panko mixture to fully cover all surfaces.

6. Add the finished pickles to the air fryer basket. Heat the fryer to 360ºF.

7. Do this in batches, spraying each layer with some cooking oil. Check the pickles after eight minutes. If not ready, add them back and cook checking every minute.

8. Serve with the ranch dressing and enjoy!

Yields: 14 Pickles

Pineapple Sticks with Yogurt

Ingredients

¼ c. desiccated coconut

½ pineapple

Ingredients for the Dip

1 cup vanilla yogurt

1 small spring fresh mint

Directions

1. Preheat the air fryer unit to 392ºF.

2. Slice the pineapple into stick segments.

3. Dip the chunks of pineapple into the coconut. It should easily stick together.

4. Arrange the sticks of pineapple into the cooker basket. Cook for ten minutes.

5. For the Dip: Dice the mint into fine bits, and add to the yogurt.

6. Pour the dip into a serving dish and decorate a plate with the baked sticks.

Yields: 4 Servings

Conclusion

Thank for making it through to the end of *Air Fryer Recipes for Quick and Healthy Meals.* Let's hope it was informative and provided you with all of the tools you need to achieve your goals, no matter what they may be.

The next step is to decide which of the tasty treats will be served first. All of them are easy to prepare with the simple guidelines provided. Why not start right now, and compile the list of everything you want to make in the first few days. You are sure to have the attention of your family when these yummy meals and snacks hit the kitchen and dining table.

With all of these new recipes, invite some friends over, and have a party. You are sure to be the hit of the neighborhood whether you choose breakfast, lunch or dinner for your menu planning. You could always have a few snacks to see if you have everyone's attention before you surprise them!

Index for Recipes

Chapter 4: Chicken Recipes

- Buffalo Chicken Wings
- Chicken Fried Rice
- Chicken Kabobs
- Chicken Kiev Supper
- Chicken Pot Pie
- Orange Chicken Wings

Chapter 5: Fish and Seafood Recipes

- Cajun Salmon
- Crumbled Fish
- Fish Tacos
- Ginger Cod Steaks
- Lemon Fish
- Salmon Patties

Chapter 6: Side Dishes

- Buffalo Cauliflower
- Button Mushroom Melt
- Grilled Corn with Feta and Lime
- Homemade Croutons
- Garlic Knots
- Stuffed Mushrooms with Sour Cream

- Twice Baked Loaded Air-Fried Potatoes

Chapter 7: Vegetable Recipes

- Broccoli

- AF Chickpeas – Ranch & Vegan Style

- Hasselback Potatoes

- Honey Roasted Carrot

- Mediterranean Vegetables

- Onion Rings

- Air Fried Potato Wedges

Chapter 8: Snacks and Appetizers

- Apple Chips

- Avocado Fries

- Cheesy Garlic Bread

- Churro Doughnut Holes

- Corn Tortilla Chips

- Crispy Fried Pickles

- Pineapple Sticks with Yogurt

** Remember to use your link to claim your 3 FREE Cookbooks on Health, Fitness & Dieting Instantly

https://bit.ly/2uS1BhB

Made in the USA
San Bernardino, CA
19 December 2018